T0246361

Baking

Introduction

This delicious collection of breads, cakes, cookies, tea breads, tray bakes and more is sure to tempt your tastebuds and appeal to a wide audience. There are recipes here that are suitable to make for any occasion including everday eating with the family, catering for school fêtes, and making a stunning centrepiece that is perfect to serve at a special occasion.

Baking is booming in popularity, an activity fuelled in part by a whole raft of light-hearted television programmes that encourage us all to don our pinnies, whip out the cookware and get creative in the kitchen.

In reality, it takes so little effort to make something delicious to eat.

Baking is a win-win activity. Not only is there great pleasure to be had in the activity of beating, blending and processing cake batter, or kneading and rolling bread and cookie dough, but the results are sure to be appreciated by everyone. And while you wait for your items to bake, the sweet and fragrant aroma of cooking that emanates from the kitchen and wafts in the air is sure to tempt the tastebuds and whet the appetite.

Here is a fabulous assortment of recipes for traditional and savoury breads to serve alongside soups, salads and main courses; sweet and salty muffins; crunchy, chewy and melt-in-the-mouth cookies; a whole range of scones on to which you can lavish butter and preserves; as well as a tempting array of cakes, tea breads and tray bakes that can be dressed up or down depending upon the occasion.

Pastry features too and there is a delightful selection of crowd-pleasing sweet and savoury confections that you can make using minimal ingredients. But before you begin there are a few instructions that you need to take note of to ensure that you get the best results for your efforts.

Bakeware

If you're starting out and just want to buy the basics, you'll find you actually need very little equipment for baking, though as your confidence and repertoire grow, so too will your desire to have a broader range of equipment. A food processor is one of the most expensive pieces of kit, though it's definitely not essential— sure it makes light work of kneading dough, or whipping up a batch of cookie dough, but you can do the job just as well by hand, using a mixing bowl and a wooden spoon. It may take a little longer, and require a little elbow grease, but many cooks prefer the good old-fashioned methods of baking, liking the feel of the batter as it is mixed and blended and knowing from experience when to beat a little more or when to add a more wet or dry ingredient to make the mix just right.

A mixing bowl is a basic requirement, but if you really are starting with nothing, you could cream cake batters and cookie doughs in a large pan (pot) instead. A wooden spoon is essential, and so is a spatula, some accurate kitchen scales and a handful of tins (pans) in which to bake your items.

With bakeware it usually follows that the more expensive the item, the better the quality you purchase. Cake tins, in particular, can make quite a difference to how an item turns out. Inexpensive tins are likely to buckle more easily, last for less time, or conduct the heat less efficiently than costly ones, so as you gain experience and learn which items you use the most you can replace the cheap items in your cupboards with better quality ones.

To start with you're most likely to need a couple of baking sheets, a square or rectangular tray bake pan for brownies, a 9 in (23 cm) deep-sided round cake tin, and a muffin tray (patty pan). Always use the correct size of tin quoted in the recipe, otherwise your cake may not bake according to the instructions.

Test your oven regularly too. It's a good idea to buy an oven thermometer and adjust your oven temperature up or down to make sure you bake at the correct temperature. Conventional ovens are hotter at the top than the base so you should always position cakes in the centre of the oven when you bake them.

If you are baking two items, one above the other on two oven shelves then swap them over half way through the baking time to ensure that both bake evenly.

Similarly if you are fitting two items side-by-side ensure that you swap the positions of each as well as turning each item around just in case your oven has hot spots and cooks unevenly. Make sure the oven shelves are level too.

Before you begin read the recipe through from start to finish and make sure you understand what to do at each stage of the recipe. Always allow sufficient time to make the goods. Once you start baking, you need to continue until the item is complete. If you break off in the middle, for instance, realising that you don't have the time to wait for the cake to bake once it is made, then the ingredients will be ruined, an expense and a waste that nobody wants.

Get all the equipment out of the cupboards that you will need and assemble them on a clean work surface. Similarly locate all of the ingredients and weigh them all out before you begin just to be doubly sure that you have them all to hand. When you weigh out the ingredients use metric, imperial or cup measurements and stick rigidly to your preferred choice. Never use a combination of the measurements because there is a slight difference in the conversions.

Note

A couple of the recipes use uncooked eggs in their creation. Never give foods containing uncooked eggs to sick or elderly people, pregnant women or young children.

Yeast & Breads

Irish Soda Bread

Makes 1 loaf

5 oz (155 g/1⅓ cups) plain (all-purpose) flour, plus extra for dusting
1 teaspoon baking soda
1 teaspoon salt
1½ oz (45 g) butter, plus extra for greasing
16 fl oz (475 ml/2 cups) buttermilk or milk

✎ Preheat oven to 400°F/200°C/Gas mark 6.

✎ Sift the flour, baking soda and salt into a mixing bowl. Rub in the butter using your fingertips, until the mixture resembles coarse breadcrumbs. Make a well in the centre of the flour mixture, pour in the milk or buttermilk and, using a round-ended knife, mix to form a soft dough.

✎ Turn the dough out onto a floured surface and knead lightly until smooth. Shape into a 7 in (18 cm) round, and place on a greased and floured baking sheet. Score the loaf into eighths using a sharp knife.

✎ Dust lightly with flour and bake for 35–40 minutes, or until the loaf sounds hollow when tapped on the base.

Wholemeal Bread

Makes 1 loaf

4 oz (115 g/1 cup) wholemeal (whole-wheat)
self-raising (self-rising) flour
4 oz (115 g/1 cup) white self-raising (self-rising) flour
½ pint (300 ml/1¼ cups) skimmed milk
oil, for greasing
1 teaspoon dry mustard (powder)
1 tablespoon sesame seeds

✎ Preheat the oven to 400°F/200°C/Gas mark 6.

✎ Sift the flour into a large bowl. Return the husks from
the sieve to the bowl. Stir in enough skimmed milk to give
a sticky dough. Knead on a lightly floured surface until
smooth, shape into a round.

✎ Place the dough on a greased baking sheet, press out
with fingers to about 1 in (2.5 cm) thick. Using a sharp knife,
mark into wedges, and cut the wedges into the dough about
½ in/12 mm deep.

✎ Sprinkle the dough with mustard and sesame seeds.
Bake for 30 minutes or until golden brown and the bread
sounds hollow on the underside when tapped.

Hot Cross Buns

Makes 18

¾ oz (21 g) dried yeast
8 fl oz (250 ml/1 cup) lukewarm milk
Pinch of salt
2 tablespoons sugar
1 teaspoon ground cinnamon (powder)
½ teaspoon ground nutmeg (powder)
¼ teaspoon mixed (apple pie) spice
2 eggs
1 lb (450 g/4 cups) plain (all purpose) flour, plus extra for dusting
2 tablespoons oil, plus extra for greasing
4 oz (115 g) dried fruit

Cross & Glaze

2 oz (55 g/½ cup) plain
(all-purpose) flour
2 tablespoons milk
2 tablespoons icing
(confectioners') sugar

🖊 Put the yeast in a large bowl. Pour in the milk and set aside in warm place for 10 minutes, or until frothy.

🖊 Stir in the salt, sugar and spices. Beat in the eggs, one at a time. Stir in half the flour to make a soft dough. Beat in the oil and continue beating for 1 minute. Knead in the remaining flour.

🖊 Place the dough in a clean, lightly oiled bowl. Turn to coat with oil. Cover with a kitchen towel and set aside in a warm place for 1 hour, or until doubled in size.

🖊 Knead the dough, working in the dried fruit on a lightly floured surface. Roll into a log. Cut into 18 even pieces.

🖊 Shape into rounds and place 1 in (2.5 cm) apart, on greased baking sheets. Cover and set aside to rise in a warm place for 20 minutes.

🖊 Preheat the oven to 400°F/200°C/Gas mark 6. To make the cross, put the flour and 2½ fl oz (75 ml/ 1/3 cup) water in a bowl. Beat until smooth. Spoon into a piping bag fitted with a plain nozzle. Pipe a cross on top of each bun.

🖊 Bake for 15 minutes or until golden. For the glaze, warm the milk and mix with the icing sugar in a bowl. Mix until smooth. Brush the glaze over the buns.

Apple Loaves

Makes 2 loaves

8 oz (225 g/2 cups) all-purpose (plain) flour, plus extra for dusting
1¾ oz (45 g/¼ cup) granulated (white) sugar, plus extra for dusting
2 teaspoons baking powder
½ teaspoon bicarbonate of soda (baking soda)
½ teaspoon salt
1½ oz (40 g) butter, chilled, plus extra for greasing
1 cooking apple, peeled and grated (shredded)
4 fl oz (120 ml/½ cup) milk, plus extra for glazing
ground cinnamon (powder), for dusting

✎ Preheat the oven to 425°F/220°C/Gas mark 7.

✎ Combine the flour, sugar, baking powder, bicarbonate of soda and salt in a large bowl. Cut in the butter until crumbly. Add the apple and milk. Stir to form a soft dough.

✎ Turn out onto a lightly floured surface. Knead gently

✎ 8–10 times. Divide into two and pat into even rounds. Place on the prepared baking sheets. Brush the tops with milk. Sprinkle with sugar, then with cinnamon. Score each top into six pie-shaped wedges.

✎ Bake for 15 minutes until browned and risen.

Country Cornbread

Makes 1 loaf

4 oz (115 g/1 cup) cornmeal (polenta)
4 oz (115 g/1 cup) plain (all-purpose) flour
2 tablespoons sugar
1 tablespoon baking powder
½ teaspoon salt
6 fl oz (175 ml/¾ cup) milk
4 fl oz (120 ml/½ cup) sour cream
2 eggs
3½ oz (100 g) butter, melted, plus extra for greasing

✎ Preheat the oven to 350°F/180°C/Gas mark 4.

✎ Grease and line a 9 in (23 cm)square cake tin (pan).

✎ Sift all the dry ingredients together into a large bowl.

✎ In another bowl, beat the melted butter, milk, cream and eggs until blended. Mix with the flour mixture until just combined.

✎ Pour the batter into the prepared tin. Bake for approximately 30 minutes, or until a skewer inserted into the centre comes out clean. Cut into squares or rectangles and serve warm.

Basil Beer Bread

Makes 1 loaf

oil, for greasing
8 oz (225 g/2 cups) self-raising (self-rising) flour, sifted
2 oz (55 g) sugar
¾ cup fresh basil, chopped
1 teaspoon crushed black peppercorns
8 fl oz (250 ml/1 cup) beer, at room temperature

✎ Preheat the oven to 350°F/180°C/Gas mark 4.

✎ Grease and line a 4 x 8 in/11 x 21 cm loaf tin (pan).

✎ Put the flour, sugar, basil, peppercorns and beer in a bowl and mix to make a soft dough.

✎ Arrange the dough in the prepared tin (pan) and bake for 50 minutes, or until bread is cooked and a skewer, when inserted into the centre, comes out clean.

✎ Leave to set in the tin for 5 minutes before turning out onto a wire rack to cool. Serve warm or cold spread with olive or sun-dried tomato paste.

Banana Bread

Makes 1 loaf

4 oz (115 g) butter, at room temperature
7 oz (225 g/1 cup) superfine (caster) sugar
2 eggs, lightly beaten
3 ripe bananas, peeled
2 tablespoons honey
2 tablespoons lemon juice
1 teaspoon vanilla extract
6 oz (150 g/1½ cups) self-rising (self-raising) flour, sifted
½ teaspoon baking soda
1 teaspoon ground cinnamon (powder)
2 oz (55 g/½ cup) almond meal (ground almonds)

✎ Preheat the oven to 350°F/180°C/Gas mark 4.

✎ Grease a 9 x 6 in (23 x 15 cm) loaf tin (pan). Put the butter and sugar in a mixing bowl. Beat with an electric beater until light and creamy. Add the eggs and beat until combined.

✎ In another bowl, combine the bananas, honey, lemon juice and vanilla and blend until smooth. Stir the banana mixture into the batter and mix until well combined. Gently fold in in the flour, baking soda, cinnamon and almonds.

✎ Tip into the prepared tin and bake for 50–60 minutes or until cooked through. Leave to set for 5 minutes then turn out on a wire rack to go cold. Serve sliced and buttered.

Blueberry Pecan Loaf

Makes 1 loaf

4 oz (115 g/1 cup) wholemeal (whole-wheat) flour
4 oz (115 g/1 cup) plain (all-purpose) flour
1½ teaspoons baking powder
1 teaspoon salt
½ teaspoon bicarbonate of soda (baking soda)
1½ oz (45 g) butter
6 fl oz (175 ml/¾ cup) natural (plain) yogurt
1 tablespoon grated lemon zest
2 eggs
4 oz (115 g/1 cup) blueberries
4 oz (115 g/1 cup) chopped pecans

Preheat the oven to 350°F/180°C/Gas mark 4. Grease and line a 1 lb (450 g) loaf tin (pan).

Sift the flours, baking powder, salt and bicarbonate of soda into the bowl of a food processor. Add the butter, and process until the mixture resembles coarse breadcrumbs.

Combine the yogurt, lemon zest and eggs in a separate bowl, mix well. Add to the processor and blend just long enough to moisten. Add the blueberries and nuts and stir through.

Tip into the prepared tin. Bake for about 1 hour, or until a skewer, when inserted into the centre comes out clean. Leave to set for a few minutes before turning out on to a wire rack to go cold.

Naan Bread

Makes 8

8 oz (225 g/1 cup) natural (plain) yogurt
8 oz (225 g/2 cups) plain (all-purpose) flour
12 oz (350 g/3 cups) wholemeal (whole-wheat)
plain (all-purpose) flour
1 tablespoon yeast
2 teaspoons salt
1 teaspoon sugar
2 tablespoon nut oil, plus extra for greasing
3 tablespoon black sesame seeds
4 oz (115 g/ ½ cup) sesame seeds

Preheat the oven to 230°C/450°F/Gas mark 8. Lightly
grease two baking sheets.

In a bowl, mix the yogurt with 12 fl oz (350 ml/ ½ cups)
boiling water and stir well. Set aside for 5 minutes.

In another bowl, mix the plain flour with 4 oz
(115 g/1 cup) of the wholemeal flour and add the yeast.
Add the yogurt mixture and stir with a wooden spoon for 3
minutes, then cover with cling film (plastic wrap).

✎ Allow to rest for 1 hour.

✎ Add the salt, sugar, oil and black sesame seeds and enough of the remaining flour to form a firm but moist dough.

✎ Begin to knead on a floured surface and continue until the dough is very silky and elastic.

✎ Allow the dough to rise in an oiled bowl for 1 hour at room temperature, or until doubled in size.

✎ Knock back (punch down) the dough and divide into 8 pieces.

✎ Shape each into a ball then flatten each into a rough circle about ½ in (12 mm) thick. Transfer to the prepared baking sheets.

✎ Brush the surface of the dough with water and sprinkle generously with sesame seeds. Cover and allow to rise for 10 minutes. Bake for 5–8 minutes.

Easy Bakes

Traditional Scones

Makes 12

8 oz (225 g/2 cups) self-rising (self-raising) flour,
plus extra for dusting
1 teaspoon baking powder
2 teaspoons sugar
1½ oz (40 g) butter, cold, plus extra for greasing
1 egg
4 fl oz (120 ml/½ cup) milk
butter and preserve, to serve

✎ Preheat the oven to 425°F/220°C/Gas mark 7.

✎ Grease and dust a baking sheet with flour. Sift together
the flour and baking powder into a large bowl. Stir in the
sugar, then rub in the butter using your fingertips, until the
mixture resembles coarse breadcrumbs.

✎ In a small bowl, whisk together the egg and milk. Make
a well in the centre of the flour mixture, pour in the egg
mixture and mix to form a soft dough. Turn onto a lightly
floured surface and knead lightly. Roll out the dough to a
¾ in (2 cm) thickness. Stamp out scones using a floured 2 in
(5 cm) cookie cutter. Arrange on the prepared baking sheet
allowing room for each to expand when baking. Brush with a
little milk then bake for 12–15 minutes, or until golden. Serve
with butter and your choice of preserve.

Date Scones

Makes 8-12

1 lb (450 g/4 cups) self-raising (self-rising) flour,
plus extra for dusting
1 teaspoon salt
2 teaspoons ground cinnamon (powder)
2 oz (55 g) butter, cold, plus extra for greasing
4 oz (115 g) dates, chopped
1 oz (30 g) sugar
16 fl oz (475 ml/2 cups) milk
1 egg beaten with 2 fl oz
(50 ml/¼ cup) milk, to glaze butter to serve

✎ Preheat the oven to 450°F/230°C/Gas mark 8.

✎ Grease and dust a baking sheet with flour.

✎ Sift the flour, salt and cinnamon into a large bowl.

✎ Add the butter and rub in using your fingertips, until the
mixture resembles coarse breadcrumbs. Add the dates and
the sugar. Make a well in the centre and add the milk all at
once, stirring quickly and lightly to form a soft dough.

✎ Turn onto a lightly floured surface and knead just enough
to make a smooth surface and roll out to ¾ in (2 cm) thick.
Stamp out rounds using a 2 in (5 cm) cookie cutter.

✎ Arrange on the baking sheet. Brush the tops with the
combined beaten egg and milk and then bake for about
10 minutes, or until golden.

Cheese Scones

Makes 12

1 lb (450 g/4 cups) self-raising (self-rising) flour,
plus extra for dusting
¼ teaspoon cayenne pepper
1 teaspoon salt
2 oz (55 g) butter, plus extra for greasing
1 tablespoon finely chopped onion
2 oz (55 g) Cheddar cheese, grated (shredded)
1 egg
¼ cup parsley, finely chopped
16 fl oz (475 ml/2 cups) milk
1 egg beaten with 2 fl oz
(50 ml/¼ cup) milk, to glaze butter, to serve

✎ Preheat the oven to 450°F/230°C/Gas mark 8.

✎ Grease and dust a baking sheet with flour. Sift the flour,
pepper and salt into a large mixing bowl, add the butter
and rub in using your fingertips until the mixture resembles
coarse breadcrumbs.

✎ Add the onion, cheese, egg and parsley and stir well.
Make a well in the centre and add the milk all at once,
stirring quickly and lightly to a soft dough.

✎ Turn onto a lightly floured surface and knead just
enough to make a smooth surface and roll out to ¾ in
(2 cm) thick. Stamp out rounds using a 2 in (5 cm) cookie
cutter.

✎ Brush the tops with the combined beaten egg and milk and
then bake for about 10 minutes, or until golden.

Coconut Macaroons

Makes 20

Oil, for greasing
5½ oz (160 g/1⅓ cups) desiccated dry unsweetened shredded)
coconut
2½ oz (65 g/⅓ cup) sugar
2 tablespoons plain
(all-purpose) flour
pinch of salt
2 egg whites, whisked
½ teaspoon almond extract

✎ Preheat the oven to 325°F/160°C/Gas mark 3.

✎ Grease and line two baking sheets.

✎ Combine the coconut, sugar, flour and salt in a bowl.

✎ In a clean, grease-free glass bowl, whisk the egg whites until soft peaks form. Gently fold in the coconut mixture with the almond extract.

✎ Drop teaspoonfuls onto the baking sheet spaced well apart. Bake for 15 minutes, or until the edges turn brown. Remove from the sheets at once and leave to cool on a wire rack.

Cheese & Bacon Muffins

Makes 12

8 oz (225 g/2 cups) self-raising (self-rising) flour
¼ teaspoon salt
1½ oz (40 g) mature
Cheddar cheese, grated (shredded)
4–5 bacon rashers (slices), fried and crumbled
1 egg
8 fl oz (250 ml/1 cup) milk
2 fl oz (50 ml/¼ cup) olive oil

✎ Preheat the oven to 400°F/200°C/Gas mark 6. Line a muffin tray with paper cases.

✎ Put the flour, baking powder, salt, cheese and bacon into a large bowl. Stir thoroughly. Make a well in the centre.

✎ In another bowl, beat the milk and oil. Pour into the well. Stir only to moisten – the batter should be lumpy. Three-quarters fill the paper cases. Bake for 20–25 minutes until golden and cooked through.

✎ Serve warm.

Pumpkin Muffins

Makes 12

6 oz (150 g/1½ cups) plain (all-purpose) flour
1 teaspoon baking powder
1 teaspoon bicarbonate of soda (baking soda)
½ teaspoon salt
½ teaspoon ground cinnamon (powder)
½ teaspoon freshly ground nutmeg
½ teaspoon ground ginger
4 oz (115 g/½ cup) raisins
1 egg
1¾ oz (45 g/¼ cup) sugar
2½ fl oz (75 ml/⅓ cup) olive oil
4½ oz (125 g/1 cup) cooked pumpkin
4 fl oz (120 ml/½ cup) milk
icing (confectioners') sugar, to dust

✎ Preheat the oven to 400°F/200°C/Gas mark 6. Line a muffin tray with paper cases.

✎ Combine the flour, baking powder, bicarbonate of soda, salt, cinnamon, nutmeg, ginger and raisins in a large bowl. Stir thoroughly. Make a well in the centre.

✎ In another bowl, beat the egg until frothy. Mix in the sugar, oil, pumpkin and milk. Pour into the well. Stir to moisten. The batter will be lumpy. Threequarters fill the paper cases, then bake for 15–20 minutes, or until golden and cooked through. Serve warm. Dust with icing sugar.

Raspberry Muffins

Makes 10

4 oz (115 g/1 cup) wholemeal (whole-wheat) self-raising (self-rising) flour
4 oz (115 g/1 cup) white self-raising (self-rising) flour
1 oz (30 g/½ cup) wheat bran
½ teaspoon (bicarbonate of soda) baking soda
1 teaspoon ground ginger
6 fl oz (175 ml/¾ cup) buttermilk
2½ fl oz (75 ml/⅓ cup) orange juice concentrate
2 eggs
4 oz (115 g/⅔ cup) fresh, or partly thawed, raspberries

✎ Preheat the oven to 350°F/180°C/Gas mark 4. Line a muffin tray with paper cases.

✎ Sift the dry ingredients into a bowl. Return any bran to the bowl. Make a well in the centre.

✎ In another bowl, beat together the buttermilk, orange juice and eggs. Pour into the well in the dry ingredients. Add the raspberries and mix until just combined – take care not to overmix. Divide between the paper cases.

✎ Bake for 20–25 minutes, or until cooked when tested with a skewer.

Peanut Butter Muffins

Makes 12

6 oz (150 g/1½ cups) plain(all-purpose) flour
1¾ oz (45 g/¼ cup) sugar
1 tablespoon baking powder
½ teaspoon salt
3½ oz (90 g/1 cup) rolled oats
8 fl oz (250 ml/1 cup) milk
1 egg
4 oz (115 g/½ cup) smooth peanut butter
2 fl oz (50 ml/¼ cup) oil

✎ Preheat the oven to 400°F/200°C/Gas mark 6. Line a muffin tray with paper cases.

✎ Combine the flour, sugar, baking powder and salt in a large bowl. Stir to mix. Make a well in the centre.

✎ Combine the oats with the milk in a medium bowl. Add the egg and peanut butter to the oats mixture and beat well. Add the oil and stir through. Pour into the well, then stir just enough to moisten.

✎ Three-quarters fill the paper cases, then bake for 15–20 minutes, or until golden and cooked through.

✎ Serve warm.

Cakes

Jaffa Pecan Cakes

Makes 12

3½ oz (100 g) dark (bittersweet) chocolate, chopped
4 oz (115 g) butter
2 eggs
2 tablespoons orange liqueur finely grated (shredded) zest of
½ orange
1¾ oz (45 g/¼ cup) caster (superfine) sugar
2 oz (60 g) pecans, chopped
2 oz (55 g/½ cup) plain (all-purpose) flour, sifted
18 pecan halves

✎ Preheat the oven to 350°F/180°C/Gas mark 4. Line two muffin trays with paper cases.

✎ Put the chopped chocolate and butter in a heatproof bowl set over a saucepan of simmering water and leave until the chocolate and butter melt, stirring occasionally. Remove the bowl from the heat and set aside to cool slightly.

✎ In a bowl, beat the eggs, then stir in the liqueur, orange zest, sugar and pecans. Fold in the chocolate mixture and mix to combine. Fold in the flour.

✎ Three-quarters fill the paper cases with batter, top with a pecan half and bake for 20 minutes, or until the cakes are cooked through. Leave to cool on a wire rack.

Pecan & Almond Cakes

Makes 12

2 eggs, separated
3½ oz (100 g/½ cup) caster (superfine) sugar
few drops vanilla extract
2 oz (55 g/½ cup plain) (all-purpose) flour
1 teaspoon baking powder
1 oz (30 g/¼ cup) mixed
pecans and almonds, chopped
2 tablespoons icing (confectioners') sugar

✎ Preheat the oven to 300°F/150°C/Gas mark 2. Line a muffin tray with paper cases.

✎ Whisk the egg yolks with the sugar in a large bowl until thick and pale. Gently stir in the vanilla. Sift the flour and baking powder over the egg and sugar mixture, then fold in.

✎ In a clean grease-free bowl, whisk the egg whites until stiff then fold gently into the egg mixture. Carefully fold the nuts into the mixture.

✎ Divide among the paper cases and bake for 15 minutes, or until golden. Dust with icing sugar and serve warm.

Victoria Sandwich Cake

Makes 1

4 eggs
5¼ oz (150 g/¾ cup) caster (superfine) sugar
4 oz (115 g/1 cup) self-raising (self-rising) flour
1 tablespoon cornflour (cornstarch)
½ oz (15 g) butter, melted
1 tablespoon icing (confectioners') sugar, sifted, for dusting

Filling

5 oz (150 g/½ cup)
strawberry jam (jelly)
4 fl oz (120 ml/½ cup)
double (heavy) cream, whipped

✎ Preheat the oven to 350°F/180°C/Gas mark 4.

✎ Grease and line two 8 in (20 cm) round cake tins (pans).

✎ Beat the eggs in a mixing bowl until thick and creamy. Gradually beat in the sugar and continue until thick and the sugar has dissolved. This will take about 10 minutes.

🖊 Sift the flour and cornflour together over the egg mixture, then fold in. Stir in 2½ fl oz (75 ml/⅓ cup warm water and the melted butter.

🖊 Divide the batter between the prepared cake tins.

🖊 Bake for 20–25 minutes, or until the cakes shrink slightly from the sides of tins and spring back when touched with the fingertips.

🖊 Stand cakes in tins for 5 minutes before turning out onto wire racks to cool.

🖊 To assemble, spread one cake with jam, then top with whipped cream and the remaining sponge cake.

🖊 Just prior to serving, dust cake with icing sugar.

Cherry & Almond Cake

Makes 1 cake

8 oz (225 g/1 cup) butter
7 oz (200 g/1 cup caster (superfine) sugar
2 eggs
8 oz (225 g/2 cups) plain (all-purpose) flour
½ teaspoon ground cinnamon (powder)
½ teaspoon ground cloves
8 oz (224 g/2 cups) ground almonds (almond meal)
1 tablespoon gin

Filling & Topping

5 tablespoons cherry jam (jelly)
8 fl oz (250 ml/1 cup) whipped cream

✎ Preheat the oven to 350°F/180°C/Gas mark 4.

✎ Grease and line an 8 in (20 cm) round deep cake tin (pan).

✎ Beat the butter until soft, add the sugar and continue beating until light and fluffy. Add the eggs, one at a time, beating well after each addition.

✎ Sift the flour, cinnamon, cloves and almonds together. Add to the creamed mixture with the gin, mixing until well combined.

✎ Tip half the batter into the prepared tin. Spread evenly with 3 tablespoons of the jam, then spread pour the remaining cake batter on top.

✎ Bake for 1 hour, or until pale golden. Leave to set in the tin for 5 minutes, then turn out onto a wire rack to cool.

✎ Spread the top of the cake with cream and decorate with the remaining jam.

Strawberry Cream Cake

Makes 1 cake

8 oz (225 g/2 cups) butter
3½ oz (100 g/½ cup) superfine (caster) sugar
2 eggs, lightly beaten
1 teaspoon vanilla extract
6 oz (150 g/1½ cups) plain (all-purpose) flour
2 oz (55 g/½ cup) cornflour (cornstarch)
1 tablespoon baking powder

Filling

8 fl oz (250 ml/1 cup) milk
½ teaspoon vanilla extract
2 oz (65 g/⅓ cup) superfine (caster) sugar
3 egg yolks
2 tablespoons cornstarch (cornflour)
8 fl oz (250 ml/1 cup) whipped cream
5 oz (150 g/1 cup) sliced strawberries, plus a handful of whole strawberries, to decorate

✎ Preheat the oven 350°F/180°C/Gas mark 4.

✎ Grease and line two 7 in (18 cm) sandwich tins (pans).

✎ In a bowl, ceam the butter and sugar until light and fluffy.

✎ Add the eggs and vanilla and beat thoroughly. Sift the flour, cornstarch and baking powder onto the egg mixture and beat well.

✎ Divide the batter between the prepared tins and bake for 20 minutes, or until cooked through.

✎ Leave to set for a few minutes, then turn out on to a wire rack to go cold.

✎ To make the custard, slowly bring the milk and vanilla to the boil in a heavy pan.

✎ Meanwhile, beat the sugar and eggs together in a bowl until the mixture is thick and creamy, and leaves a trail when the beaters are lifted.

🖊 Fold in the cornstarch. Then pour the hot milk onto the egg mixture, beating well.

🖊 Return the mixture to the pan and reheat, stirring constantly.

🖊 Boil for 1 minute, then pour into a bowl and cover with a sheet of baking paper until cold.

🖊 Spread the custard on one cake.

🖊 Top with sliced strawberries and some of the cream.

🖊 Add the other cake and decorate with strawberries and cream.

Coffee Sandwich Cake

Makes 1 cake

9 oz (250 g) butter, at room temperature
7 oz (225 g/1 cup) caster (superfine) sugar
6 eggs, lightly beaten
8 oz (225 g/2 cups) self-raising (self-rising) flour, sifted

Icing

2¼ oz (60 g) butter, softened
3 oz (85 g/¾ cup) icing (confectioners') sugar, sifted
½ teaspoon ground cinnamon powder
2 teaspoons instant coffee
dissolved in 2 teaspoons hot water, then cooled

Filling

1 tablespoon coffee-flavoured liqueur
4 fl oz (120 ml/½ cup) double (heavy) cream, whipped

↘ Preheat the oven to 325°F/160°C/Gas mark 3.

↘ Grease and line two 7 in (18 cm) sandwich tins (pans).

↘ Cream the butter and sugar in a large bowl until light and fluffy. Add the eggs, one at a time and beat well. Sift over the flour and mix to combine.

↘ Divide the batter between the prepared tins and bake for 30-35 minutes, or until golden.

↘ Leave to set in the tin for a few minuts then turn out on to a wire rack to go cold.

↘ Meanwhile, to make the icing, beat the butter, icing sugar, cinnamon and coffee in a large bowl until light and fluffy.

↘ To make the filling, fold the liqueur into the whipped cream.

↘ Spread the filling over one cake and top with the remaining cake.

↘ Spread the icing over the top of the cake.

Chocolate Caramel Cheesecake

Makes 1 cake

Base

5 oz (150 g) digestive biscuits, finely crushed
1¾ oz (50 g) butter, melted

Filling

¼ cup evaporated milk
13 oz (380 g) canned caramel
1 cup pecan nuts, chopped
17 oz (500 g) cream cheese
½ cup sugar
2 eggs
1 teaspoon vanilla essence
¾ cup chocolate chips, melted
Preheat oven to 350°F (180°C).

Base

✎ Combine the crumbs and melted butter. Press mixture evenly into a 9 in (23 cm) springform tin. Bake for 8 minutes. Remove from oven and allow to cool.

Filling

🥄 Combine milk and caramel in a heavy-based saucepan.

🥄 Cook over low heat until melted, stirring often. Pour over biscuit base. Sprinkle pecans evenly over caramel layer and set aside.

🥄 Beat cream cheese at high speed with electric mixer until light and fluffy.

🥄 Gradually add sugar, mixing well. Add eggs one at a time, beating well after each addition.

🥄 Stir in vanilla and melted chocolate, beat until blended. Pour over pecan layer.

🥄 Bake for 30 minutes.

🥄 Remove from oven and run knife around edge of tin to release sides. Cool to room temperature.

🥄 Cover and chill for 8 hours.

🥄 Decorate with a chopped flaky chocolate bar and chopped jersey caramels. Serve with whipped cream.

Key Lime Cheesecake

Serves 12

Base

5 oz (150 g) digestive biscuits, finely crushed
2 tablespoons sugar
1¾ oz (50 g) butter, melted

Filling

19 oz (570 g) cream cheese, softened
¾ cup sugar
1 cup sour cream
3 tablespoons plain (all-purpose) flour
3 large eggs
¾ cup fresh lime juice
1 teaspoon vanilla essence

Candied Lime

1 cup water
1½ cups caster (superfine) sugar
3–4 fresh limes, thinly sliced

✎ Preheat oven to 375°F (190°C).

Base

✎ In a bowl, combine the crumbs and sugar, then stir in the butter well. Pat the mixture evenly onto the bottom and ¼in (1cm) up the sides of a buttered 10in (25cm) springform tin.

✎ Bake the base in the centre of the oven for 8 minutes.

✎ Transfer the pan to a rack and set aside to cool.

Filling

✎ Beat together the cream cheese and sugar with an electric mixer until smooth. Beat in the sour cream and flour, then add the eggs one at a time, beating well after each addition.

✎ Add the lime juice and vanilla, and beat until smooth.

✎ Pour the filling over the base. Bake for 15 minutes, reduce the temperature to 250°F (120°C) and bake for 50-55 minutes more, or until the centre is barely set.

✎ Allow to cool on a rack, then refrigerate, covered, overnight.

✎ Remove the cheesecake from the tin and transfer it to a plate.

Candied lime

✎ Place the water and 1 cup of the sugar in a pan. Boil until the sugar dissolves.

✎ Add the lime slices and simmer for 10 minutes.

✎ Meanwhile place the rest of the sugar on a tray.

✎ Remove the limes from the heat, strain and dry on absorbent paper.

✎ Cool slightly, then place one at a time on the tray of sugar to coat.

✎ Place around the edge of the cheesecake and serve.

New York-Style Cheesecake

Serves 6-8

Base

4 oz (120 g) digestive biscuits, finely crushed
¾ cup sugar
1¾ oz (50 g) butter, melted

Filling

1½ cups sour cream
1 cup sugar
2 eggs
1 teaspoon vanilla essence
17 oz (500 g) cream cheese, broken into small pieces
1½ oz (40 g) butter, melted

✎ Preheat oven to 330°F (165°C).

Base

✎ Blend the biscuit crumbs, sugar and melted butter, then line the bottom of an ungreased 9 in (23cm) springform tin.

Filling

✎ Blend the sour cream, sugar, eggs and vanilla in a food processor for 1 minute. Add the cream cheese, blend until smooth. While blending, pour the melted butter through the top of the machine. Pour cream cheese mixture into the springform tin. Bake in the lower third of the oven for 45 minutes, remove from oven and cool.

✎ Refrigerate for 4 hours, preferably overnight. Dust with plenty of icing sugar before cutting and serving. Serve with whipped cream.

Cookies

Cinnamon Cookies

Makes 24

8 oz (225 g) butter, softened, plus extra for greasing
4 oz (115 g) caster
(superfine) sugar
1 teaspoon vanilla extract
12 oz (350 g/3 cups) plain (all-purpose) flour
2 teaspoons ground cinnamon (powder)
salt
6 oz (150 g/1½ cups) icing (confectioners') sugar

\ In a bowl, beat together the butter, sugar and vanilla extract. Stir in the flour, 1 teaspoon of cinnamon and a pinch of salt to make a soft dough. Cover and refrigerate for 1 hour.

\ Preheat oven to 350°F/180°C/Gas mark 4. Grease two baking sheets.

\ Form mixture into 1 in (2.5 cm) balls and place on a prepared baking sheet, leaving space between each one. Bake for 15 minutes.

\ Leave to set on the baking sheets for a few minutes, then transfer to a wire rack to cool.

\ Mix together the icing sugar and remaining cinnamon and dust over the cookies before serving.

Coffee Kisses

Makes 24

9 oz (250 g) butter, at room temperature, plus extra for greasing
2 oz (55 g/½ cup) icing (confectioners') sugar, sifted, plus extra for dusting
2 teaspoons instant coffee powder or granules dissolved in 1 tablespoon hot water, then cooled
8 oz (225 g/2 cups) plain (all-purpose) flour, sifted
2 oz (55 g) dark (bittersweet) chocolate, melted

✎ Preheat the oven to 350°F/180°C/Gas mark 4.

✎ Grease two baking sheets.

✎ Beat the butter and icing sugar together in a mixing bowl until light and fluffy. Stir in the coffee and then the flour.

✎ Spoon the mixture into a piping bag fitted with a medium star nozzle and pipe ¾ in (2 cm) rounds of mixture ¾ in (2 cm) apart on the prepared baking sheets.

✎ Bake for 10–12 minutes, or until lightly browned. Leave to set for 5 minutes before turning out onto a wire rack to cool completely.

✎ Join the cookies with a little melted chocolate, then dust with icing sugar.

Almond Biscotti

Makes 30

oil, for greasing
2 large eggs
3½ oz (100 g/½ cup) caster (superfine) sugar
1 teaspoon vanilla extract
1 teaspoon grated orange zest
6½ oz (180 g/1²/₃ cups) plain (all-purpose) flour, plus extra for dusting
½ teaspoon baking powder
¾ cup blanched almonds, lightly toasted
egg white, for glazing

✎ Preheat the oven to 350°F/180°C/Gas mark 4.

✎ Grease two baking sheets and dust with flour. In a mixing bowl, beat the eggs, sugar, vanilla extract and orange zest until thick and creamy. Sift the flour and baking powder into the egg mixture and fold in with the almonds.

✎ Knead on a floured surface until smooth. Divide dough in half. Shape each piece into a log about 2 in (5 cm) wide and 1 in (2. 5cm) thick. Place on a baking sheet. Brush with egg white. Bake for 30 minutes, or until firm. Cool for 10 minutes. Cut each log diagonally into ³/₈ in (1 cm) thick slices.

✎ Place on the baking trays. Bake for 20–30 minutes, or until dry and crisp. Cool on wire racks.

Florentines

Makes 20

4 oz (115 g/½ cup) butter, at room temperature
3½ oz (100 g/½ cup) sugar
5 tablespoons golden (light corn) syrup
1 oz (30 g/¼ cup) plain (all-purpose) flour
4 oz (115 g/1 cup) sliced (flaked) almonds
4 oz (115 g/½ cup) glacé cherries, chopped
2 oz (55 g/½ cup) walnuts, chopped
1½ oz (40 g/¼ cup) mixed peel, chopped
5 oz (150 g) milk chocolate

✎ Preheat the oven to 350°F/180°C/Gas mark 4.

✎ Line four baking sheets with baking paper. Cream the butter and sugar in a large bowl untilsoft and fluffy. Beat in the golden syrup. Sift in the flour an stir to combine. Add the almonds, cherries, walnuts and mixed peel and mix well.

✎ Place tablespoonfuls of the mixture onto the prepared baking sheets, leaving plenty of room for the cookies to spread. Using a knife, press each one out as flat and round as possible. Cook no more than 4 or 5 to a tray.

✎ Bake for 10 minutes, or until golden brown. Leave to set for 5 minutes before transferring to a wire rack to go cold. Meanwhile, melt the chocolate in a bowl set over a pan (pot) of simmering water. When the florentines are cold, coat with melted chocolate on their flat sides.

Peanut Butter & Honey Cookies

Makes 30

5¼ oz (150 g/¾ cup) crunchy peanut butter
5½ oz (160 g/⅔ cup honey
1 egg, lightly beaten
4 oz (115 g/1 cup) plain (all-purpose) flour, sifted
1¾ oz (50 g/½ cup) rolled oats
2 oz (55 g/⅓ cup) sultanas (golden raisins)

✎ Preheat the oven to 325°F/160°C/Gas mark 3. Line two or three baking sheets with baking paper.

✎ Put the peanut butter and honey in a saucepan and place over gentle heat. Stir until soft and combined.

✎ Leave to coool slightly then stir in the beaten egg.

✎ Fold in the remaining ingredients. Shape teaspoons of mixture into balls.

✎ Arrange on the prepared trays leaving space between each. Press lightly with a fork. Bake for 12 minutes, or until golden.

✎ Leave to set for a few minutes before turning out onto a wire rack to go cold.

Tray Bakes

Choc-mint Brownies

Makes 30

4 oz (115 g/½ cup) butter
7 oz (200 g) dark (bittersweet) chocolate, broken into pieces
2 eggs
6 oz (175 g/¾ cup) brown sugar
2 tablespoons unsweetened cocoa powder
4 oz (115 g/1 cup) all-purpose (plain) flour
2 tablespoons vegetable oil

Topping

4 oz (115 g/1 cup)
(confectioners') sugar
½ oz (15 g) butter
3 drops peppermint extract

↘ Preheat the oven to 325°F/160°C/Gas mark 3.

↘ Grease and line a 9 in (23 cm) square tin (pan).

↘ Melt the butter and chocolate in a medium saucepan, stir occasionally.

↘ Leave to cool slightly.

↘ Beat the eggs and sugar in a large bowl until light and creamy. Beat in the cocoa, flour and the oil, then the cooled chocolate mixture.

↘ Pour the batter mixture into the prepared cake tin.

↘ Bake for 40 minutes, or until a skewer inserted into the centre comes out clean. Turn out onto a wire rack to go cold.

↘ To make the topping, sift the icing sugar into a heatproof bowl, add the butter and peppermint extract, and stir over simmering water until smooth.

↘ Drizzle or pipe the topping over the brownies.

↘ Cut into squares.

Brownies

Makes 20

5 oz (150 g) butter, softened
4 fl oz (120 ml/½ cup) honey, warmed
2 eggs, lightly beaten
7 oz (200 g/1¾ cups) self-raising (self-rising) flour, sifted
5¼ oz (160 g/⅔ cup) brown sugar
4 oz (115 g) dark chocolate, melted and cooled
icing (confectioners') sugar, sifted, for dusting

✎ Preheat the oven to 350°F/180°C/Gas mark 4.

✎ Grease and line a 9 in (23 cm) square tin (pan). Put the butter, honey, eggs, flour, brown sugar, melted chocolate and 1 tablespoon of water in a food processor and process until the ingredients are combined.

✎ Tip the batter the prepared cake tin. Bake for 30–35 minutes, or until a skewer, when inserted in the cake centre, comes out clean.

✎ Leave to set in the tin for 5 minutes before turning out onto a wire rack to cool completely.

✎ Dust with icing sugar and cut into squares.

Caramel Squares

Makes 20

3½ oz (100 g) butter, plus extra for greasing
1½ oz (40 g) sugar
3 oz (85 g/¾ cup) cornflour (cornstarch), sifted
3 oz (85 g/¾ cup) plain (all-purpose) flour, sifted,
plus extra for dusting

Filling & topping

4 oz (115 g/½ cup) butter
4 oz (115 g/½ cup) brown sugar
2 tablespoons honey
14 oz (400 g) can sweetened condensed milk
1 teaspoon vanilla extract
7 oz (200 g) dark (semisweet) chocolate, melted
Preheat the oven to 350°F/180°C/Gas mark 4.

Grease and line a 8 x 12 in (20 x 30cm) shallow cake tin (pan).

To make the base, beat the butter and sugar in a mixing bowl until light and fluffy.

Mix in the cornflour and flour.

Turn out onto a lightly floured surface and knead briefly, then press into the prepard tin and bake for 25 minutes or until firm.

To make the filling, put the butter, brown sugar and honey in a saucepan and melt over medium heat, stirring constantly until the sugar dissolves and the ingredients are combined.

Bring to the boil and simmer for 7 minutes.

Beat in the condensed milk and vanilla extract. Pour the filling over the base and bake for 20 minutes. Set aside to cool completely.

Spread melted chocolate over the filling. Set aside until firm, then cut into squares.

Chocolate Rum Slices

Makes 24

4 oz (115 g/1 cup) self-raising (self-rising) flour, sifted
1 tablespoon unsweetened cocoa powder, sifted
3½ oz (100 g/½ cup) caster (superfine) sugar
2½ oz (65 g) desiccated (dry unsweetened shredded)
coconut, plus extra for dusting
2½ oz (65 g) raisins, chopped
4 oz (115 g/½ cup) butter, melted
1 teaspoon rum
2 tablespoons dark (semisweet) chocolate, grated (shredded)
2 eggs, lightly beaten

Topping

4 oz (115 g/1 cup) icing (confectioners') sugar
2 tablespoons unsweetened cocoa powder
½ oz (15 g) butter, softened

✎ Preheat the oven to 350°F/180°C/Gas mark 4.

✎ Grease and line a 10 in (25 cm) square cake tin (pan).

✎ Put the flour, cocoa powder, sugar, coconut and raisins in a bowl and mix to combine.

✎ Stir in the melted butter, rum, grated chocolate and beaten eggs. Mix well to thoroughly combine.

✎ Press the batter into the prepared tin and bake for 20–25 minutes, or until firm.

✎ Allow to cool in the tin.

✎ To make the topping, sift the icing sugar and cocoa together into a bowl. Add the butter and 1 tablespoon boiling water, and beat to a spreadable consistency.

✎ Turn the bake out onto a wire rack, spread with topping and dust with extra coconut.

✎ Refrigerate until firm, then cut into squares.

Walnut Chocolate Slice

Makes 24

4 egg whites
1¾ oz (45 g/¼ cup) sugar
4 oz (115 g) chocolate, melted and cooled
3 oz (85 g) butter, melted and cooled
1½ teaspoons vanilla extract
4 oz (115 g/1 cup) plain (all-purpose) flour
2 oz (55 g/¼ cup) brown sugar
5 oz (160 g/⅓ cup) unsweetened cocoa powder
2 teaspoons baking powder
½ teaspoon bicarbonate ofsoda (baking soda)
1½ oz (40 g/⅓ cup) chopped
walnuts or pecans

✎ Preheat the oven to 375°F/190°C/Gas mark 5. Grease and line a 9 in (23 cm) deep-sided square tin(pan).

✎ Whisk the egg whites in a clearn grease-free bowl until soft peaks form. Gradually beat in the sugar. and continue until it dissolves. Fold in the melted chocolate and butter and the vanilla extract. Into a large bowl sift the flour, brown sugar, cocoa, baking powder and bicarbonate of soda. Make a well in the centre. Fold in the egg whites and walnuts until just combined. Tip into the prepared tin and smooth out to the corners.

✎ Bake for 20-25 minutes, or until cooked when tested with a skewer. Cool in the pan. Cut into 1½-2 in (4-5 cm) squares.

Raspberry Yogurt Slice

Makes 14

3½ oz (100 g) butter
4 oz (115 g/1 cup) plain (all-purpose) flour
2 oz (55 g/¼ cup) brown sugar
3 oz (80 g/¾ cup) rolled oats

Topping

4 oz (115 g) cream cheese
6 fl oz (175 ml/¾ cup) raspberry-flavoured yogurt
1 tablespoon honey
1 teaspoon lemon juice
1 teaspoon grated lemon zest
1 tablespoon gelatine powder
8 oz (225 g) frozenraspberries, thawed
1¾ oz (45 g/¼ cup) sugar

✎ Preheat the oven to 350°F/180°C/Gas mark 4.

✎ Grease and line a deep-sided 11 x 7 in (28 x 18 cm) baking tray.

✎ Blend the butter and flour together in a food processor with the sugar until the dough just comes together. Fold in the oats.

✎ Press into the base of the prepared tray. Bake for about 15–20 minutes, or until a skewer comes out clean, then allow to cool.

✎ Beat the cream cheese with the yogurt and honey. Add the lemon juice and zest.

✎ Scatter the gelatine over 2 fl oz (50 ml/¼ cup) water to soften.

✎ Heat three-quarters of the raspberries in a pan and add the sugar and softened gelatine. Bring to the boil, stirring until the sugar and gelatine have thoroughly dissolved. Press through a sieve (strainer), then leave to cool to egg white consistency. Stir into the cheese and yogurt mixture with the remaining raspberries.

✎ Pour the yogurt mixture over the base and refrigerate overnight. Serve with extra raspberries.

Pumpkin Nut Slice

Makes 6-8

6 oz (175 g/¾ cup) butter
7 oz (200 g/1 cup) caster (superfine) sugar
4 oz (115 g/1 cup) plain (all-purpose) flour
1 ½ teaspoon baking powder
1½ teaspoons ground cinnamon powder
½ teaspoon mixed (apple pie) spice
2 eggs, lightly beaten
2 oz (55 g/½ cup) chopped pecans or walnuts
½ teaspoon vanilla extract
3 oz (85 g/½ cup) chopped raisins
5½ oz (165 g/1 cup) drained, crushed pineapple
4 oz (115 g/¾ cup) cooked, mashed pumpkin

Topping

6 oz (150 g/1½ cups) icing (confectioners') sugar
8 oz (225 g) cream cheese, softened
½ teaspoon vanilla extract
2 teaspoons lemon juice

✎ Preheat the oven to 350°F/180°C/Gas mark 4.

✎ Grease and line a 9 in (23 cm) square tin (pan).

✎ Beat the butter and sugar in a large bowl until light and fluffy.

✎ Sift the flour, baking powder and spices over and stir to blend. Beat in the beaten eggs.

✎ Stir in the nuts, vanilla extract, raisins, pineapple and pumpkin. Mix well and pour into the prepared tin.

✎ Bake for 1 hour, or until a skewer inserted in the centre of the cake comes out clean.

✎ Leave to set for a few minutes before turning out on to a wire rack to go cold.

✎ To make the icing, place all the ingredients in a mixing bowl and beat until well combined, then increase speed and beat until light and fluffy.

✎ Spread icing over the cake.

Pies and Tarts

Individual Meat Pies

Makes 8

1 lb 11 oz (750 g) shortcrust pastry
13 oz (375 g) puff pastry
1 egg, lightly beaten

Filling

1 lb 11 oz (750 g) lean minced (ground) beef
16 fl oz (475 ml/2 cups) beef stock
freshly ground black pepper
2 tablespoons cornflour (cornstarch), blended with 4 fl oz
(120 ml/½ cup) water
1 tablespoon Worcestershire sauce
1 teaspoon soy sauce

✎ Preheat the oven to 425°F/220°C/Gas mark 7.

✎ To make the filling, heat a frying pan over a medium
heat, add the meat and cook until brown.

✎ Drain off the juices, stir in the stock, season with black
pepper, to taste, and bring to the boil. Reduce the heat,
cover and simmer for 20 minutes.

✎ Stir in the cornflour mixture, Worcestershire and soy sauces and cook, stirring, until the mixture boils and thickens. Cool.

✎ Roll out the shortcrust pastry to ¼ in (5 mm) thick and use to line the base and sides of eight buttered, small metal pie dishes.

✎ Roll out the puff pastry to ¼ in (5 mm) thick and cut out rounds to fit the top of the pies.

✎ Divide the filling between the pie dishes.

✎ Brush the edges of the shortcrust pastry with water, top with rounds of puff pastry and press the edges together to seal.

✎ Brush the pies with egg and bake for 5 minutes, then reduce the oven temperature to 350°F/180°C/Gas mark 4 and bake for another 10-15 minutes, or until pastry is golden.

Potato, Egg & Leek Pies

Makes 10

1 lb (450 g) shortcrust pastry filling
1 oz (30 g) butter
4 leeks, sliced
2 cloves garlic, crushed
2 teaspoons curry powder
6 potatoes, cooked until tender and diced
10½ oz (290 g) asparagus, stalks removed, blanched and chopped
4 hard boiled eggs, diced
4 oz (115 g) mature Cheddar cheese, grated (shredded)
¼ cup fresh parsley, chopped
¼ pint (150 ml/⅔) cup sour cream
1 egg and 2 yolks, lightly beaten, plus 1 egg for glazing
freshly ground black pepper
1 tablespoon caraway seeds

Preheat the oven to 425°F/220°C/Gas mark 7.

To make the filling, melt the butter in a frying pan over a low heat, add the leeks and cook for 3-4 minutes, or until soft. Increase the heat to medium, stir in the garlic and curry powder and cook for 1 minute.

In a bowl, combine the potatoes, leek mixture, asparagus, eggs, cheese, parsley, sour cream and black pepper, to taste. Set aside.

Meanwhile roll out the shortcrust to $1/5$ in (5 mm) thick, and cut to fit the base and sides of ten buttered, metal pie dishes.

Cut the remaining pastry to fit the top of the pies.

Spoon the filling into the pie dishes, brush the pastry edges with beaten egg and top with pie lids. Press the pastry edges together, to seal.

Using a sharp knife, make a slit on the top of each pie, then brush with beaten egg and dust with caraway seeds.

Bake for 15 minutes.

Reduce the oven temperature to 350°F/180°C/Gas mark 4 and bake for 15 minutes, or until golden.

Leek & Apple Pie

Makes 1 pie

13 oz (370 g) shortcrust pastry

Leek Filling

1 tablespoon butter
1 cooking apple, cored, peeled and sliced
3 small leeks, sliced
4 rashers (strips) bacon, chopped
¼ teaspoon ground cloves
¼ teaspoon ground nutmeg
2 oz (55 g) blue cheese, crumbled
3 eggs, lightly beaten
6 fl oz (175 ml/¾ cup)
double (heavy) cream
2 tablespoons port (optional)
freshly ground black pepper

↘ Preheat the oven to 425°F/220°C/Gas mark 7.

↘ To make the filling, melt the butter in a frying pan and cook the apple, leeks and bacon over a medium heat for 5–8 minutes, or until apple softens.

↘ Add the cloves and nutmeg and cook for 1 minute longer.

↘ Set aside to cool.

↘ Roll out the pastry on a lightly floured surface and line the base and sides of a lightly greased 9 in (23 cm) flan tin (pan).

↘ Prick the base of the pastry with a fork, line with baking paper and half-fill with baking beans. Bake for 10 minutes.

↘ Remove the beans and paper.

↘ Reduce the oven temperature to 350°F/180°C/Gas mark 4.

↘ Spread the apple mixture over the base of the pastry case.

↘ In a bowl, mix the cheese, eggs, cream, port (if using) and black pepper, to taste, to combine and carefully pour into the pastry case.

↘ Bake for 30–35 minutes, or until pie is firm.

Rhubarb & Apple Tart

Makes 1 tart

4 oz (115 g/1 cup) plain (all-purpose) flour, sifted, plus extra for dusting
2 teaspoons icing sugar, sifted
3 oz (85 g) butter, chilled and diced, plus extra for greasing

Filling

6 stalks rhubarb, chopped
3 oz (90 g) sugar
1 oz (30 g) butter
3 cooking apples, cored, peeled and sliced
4 oz (115 g) cream cheese
1 teaspoon vanilla extract
1 egg

✎ To make the pastry, put the flour and icing sugar in a large bowl and rub in the butter, using your fingertips, until the mixture resembles coarse breadcrumbs. Add 4 teaspoons iced water and knead to a smooth dough.

✎ Wrap in cling film (plastic wrap) and refrigerate for 30 minutes.

✎ Preheat the oven to 400°F/200°C/Gas mark 6.

✎ Roll out the pastry on a lightly floured surface and use to line a buttered 9 in (23 cm) fluted flan tin. Line the pastry case with baking paper and baking beans. Bake for 15 minutes.

✎ Remove the beans and paper and cook for 5 minutes longer. Reduce the oven temperature to 350°F/180°C/Gas mark 4.

✎ To make the filling, poach the rhubarb until tender. Drain then stir in 2 tablespoons of the sugar and set aside to cool.

✎ Melt the butter in a frying pan and cook the apples for 3-4 minutes. Set aside to cool. Place cream cheese, rest of the sugar, vanilla and egg in a bowl and beat until smooth.

✎ Spoon the rhubarb into pastry case, top with cream cheese mixture and arrange the apple slices on top.

✎ Bake for 40-45 minutes, or until filling is firm.

Apple Chiffon Tart

Makes 1 Tart

13 oz (370 g) shortcrust pastry

Filling & topping

4 teaspoons gelatine powder
2 large cooking apples, peeled, cored and diced
2 egg whites
1 tablespoon caster (superfine) sugar
8 fl oz (250 ml/1 cup) double (heavy) cream
1½ oz (40 g/½ cup) dessicated (dry unsweetened shredded) coconut
2 oz (55 g/¼ cup) brown sugar

☴ Preheat the oven to 400°F/200°C/Gas mark 6.

☴ Roll out the pastry on a lightly floured surface and use to line a buttered 9 in (23 cm) fluted flan tin.

☴ Line the pastry case with baking paper and baking beans. Bake for 15 minutes.

☴ Remove the beans and paper and cook for 5 minutes longer. Leave to cool.

✎ Put the apples in a small pan with a drizzle of water and cook over medium heat until soft and puréed. Leave to go cold. Set aside quarter of the purée. Add the gelatine to 2 fl oz 50 ml (¼ cup) hot water and stir briskly with a fork until dissolved. Stir in to the large quantity of apple purée.

✎ In a bowl, whisk the egg whites until stiff. Gradually whisk in the sugar. Fold in half the cream then tip into the apple mixture. Mix to combine. Pour into the pastry case. Chill until set.

✎ Spread the remaining apple purée over the top of the tart.

✎ Scatter the coconut and brown sugar on top.

✎ Whip the remaining cream and pipe around the edge.

Index

First published in 2023 by New Holland Publishers, Sydney
Level 1, 178 Fox Valley Road, Wahroonga, 2076, NSW, Australia

newhollandpublishers.com

A record of this book is held at the National Library of Australia

ISBN : 9781760795856

Group Managing Director: Fiona Schultz
Designer: Ben Taylor (Taylor Design)
Production Director: Arlene Gippert

Printed in China

10 9 8 7 6 5 4 3 2 1

Keep up with New Holland Publishers

 NewHollandPublishers

 @newhollandpublishers